18.95

D1519907

The *Incredible* Quest to Find the *Titanic*

Brad Matsen

Enslow Publishers, Inc.

40 Industrial Road	PO Box 38
Box 398	Aldershot
Berkeley Heights, NJ 07922	Hants GU12 6BP
USA	UK

http://www.enslow.com

Library of Congress Cataloging-in-Publication Data

Matsen, Bradford.
　The incredible quest to find the Titanic / Brad Matsen.
　　p. cm. — (Incredible deep-sea adventures)
　　Summary: An account of the sinking of the Titanic and Robert Ballard's search
for the wreckage.
　　Includes bibliographical references (p.) and index.
　　ISBN 0-7660-2191-2 (hardcover)
　　1. Titanic (Steamship)—Juvenile literature. 2. Shipwrecks—North Atlantic
Ocean—Juvenile literature. 3. Underwater exploration—North Atlantic Ocean—
Juvenile literature. 4. Ballard, Robert D.—Juvenile literature. [1. Titanic
(Steamship) 2. Shipwrecks. 3. Ballard, Robert D.] I. Title.
　G530.T6 M34 2003
　910'.91634—dc21
　　　　　　　　　　　　　　　　　　　　2002153920
Printed in the United States of America

10 9 8 7 6 5 4 3 2 1

To Our Readers: We have done our best to make sure all Internet Addresses in this book
were active and appropriate when we went to press. However, the author and the
publisher have no control over and assume no liability for the material available on those
Internet sites or on other Web sites they may link to. Any comments or suggestions can
be sent by e-mail to comments@enslow.com or to the address on the back cover.

Photo Credits: © 1999 Artville, LLC, p. 24; Emory Kristof/National Geographic
Society Image Collection, pp. 8, 10, 23, 29, 30–31, 33; Copyright RMS Titanic, Inc., p.
42; Six Titanic Paintings Cards, John Batchelor, Dover Publications, Inc., pp. 1, 4, 5, 12,
14, 18, 20–21, 22, 35, 38, 40, 44–48; Story of the "Titanic" Cards, Frank O. Braynard,
Dover Publications, Inc., pp. 3, 13, 34; © Woods Hole Oceanographic Institution, pp. 7,
26, 37, 41.

Cover Photos: National Oceanic and Atmospheric Association (top left); Six Titanic
Paintings Cards, John Batchelor, Dover Publications, Inc. (top right); Story of the
"Titanic" Cards, Frank O. Braynard, Dover Publications, Inc. (bottom).

Contents

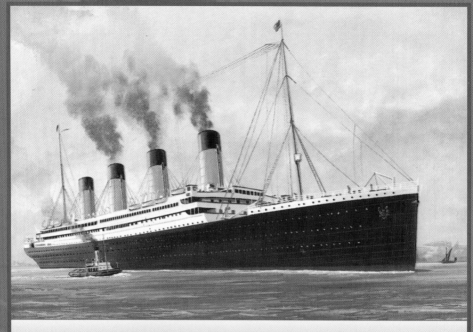

ON APRIL 10, 1912, THE *TITANIC* SET SAIL FROM ENGLAND. IT WAS THE LARGEST SHIP IN THE WORLD AT THAT TIME.

CHAPTER 1

Searching
for
Titanic

Titanic was the biggest ship in the world when it made its first voyage from Southampton, England, bound for New York City, U.S.A. Its passengers and crew thought it was unsinkable. But on the night of April 14, 1912, the *Titanic* hit an iceberg in the cold North Atlantic. Two hours and forty minutes later, it broke in half. *Titanic* then plunged more than two miles to the bottom of the sea. Only 712 people were saved. The other 1,497 died.[1]

Two mysteries surrounded the greatest shipwreck of all time. The first mystery was: Where was the *Titanic*? The second: How did the "unsinkable" ship sink?

Seventy-three years after *Titanic* disappeared into the sea, Robert Ballard and Jean-Louis Michel were trying to solve the mysteries. Finding the most famous shipwreck in history was a lifelong dream for the two scientists. For years, they had studied charts and planned the expedition to find *Titanic*.

In the early summer of 1985, Michel led an expedition to search the ocean floor. Using underwater sonar, they checked the area where they thought the wreck might be. A sonar device sends out sound waves that can be reflected by objects on the ocean floor. The signal bounces back to the scientists on the surface, where it can be studied. Michel could not tell exactly where the *Titanic* was, but the sonar maps did show them where there was only mud and sand on the bottom.

Later that summer, Ballard and Michel were using the sonar maps to try to actually find *Titanic*. By August, they had been searching for five long weeks. They were using a remote-controlled machine named *Argo* for their hunt.

Argo was towed on a cable behind the research ship *Knorr*. The cable stretched more than two miles down to the bottom of the ocean. *Argo* was piloted from a control room on *Knorr*. *Argo* carried cameras that sent pictures to the ship.[2]

Other people had tried to find the famous wreck and failed. Robert Ballard and Jean-Louis Michel knew the general area where *Titanic* went down. But the ocean is so vast, they did not know exactly where to find the wreck of the great ship. They were using a search pattern to try to cover

ROBERT BALLARD AND JEAN-LOUIS MICHEL SEARCHED FOR THE SUNKEN *TITANIC* FROM THE RESEARCH SHIP *KNORR*.

the area where they hoped to find *Titanic*. In a few days, they had to return to port. They were running out of time.

Late Nights and Tired Eyes

The search continued. The lights in the control room were very dim. Two crew members sat in front of six display monitors. Some of the monitors showed the *Argo*'s position in the sea. Others showed the pictures from *Argo*'s five video cameras. One of the crew members piloted *Argo* with a remote control. It was like a joystick for controlling a computer game.

The pictures from the bottom showed mostly light brown mud. The crew kept its spirits up by listening to music. They watched the monitors in four-hour shifts, twenty-four hours a day. After five weeks of searching, they were tired and restless. Most of all, they were afraid they would not find the *Titanic*.[3]

With strained eyes, they stared at the monitors. They saw sea cucumbers, starfish, and boulders left by melting icebergs. They had several false alarms, too. Once, they saw a huge mound and thought it could be a ship. When they

IN THE CONTROL ROOM OF *KNORR*, JEAN-LOUIS MICHEL (FAR RIGHT) AND ROBERT BALLARD (SECOND FROM RIGHT) STUDY THE VIDEO SCREEN DURING A RUN BY THE UNDERWATER SEARCH VEHICLE *ARGO*.

zoomed in with *Argo*'s cameras, they found it was only a pile of sand. There was still no sign of *Titanic*.

First Sign of *Titanic*

At one o'clock in the morning on September 1, Bill Lange, Stu Harris, Jean-Louis Michel, and the other members of the night crew were on duty. Everyone was watching the monitors. They wondered how they would keep themselves awake for another night. Robert Ballard was off duty, reading in his cabin.

Argo was cruising just above the bottom of the sea. Music played softly on the control room speakers. Jean-Louis Michel said, "There's something." He pointed at one of the monitors. Suddenly, everyone in the control room was alert. There was a large hump on the bottom. Would it be another false alarm? Harris zoomed in with the camera. "It's coming in," he said. A few seconds later, Lange cried, "Wreckage!"[4]

"Let's go get Bob," Harris said.[5]

Titanic Is Found

Ballard rushed to the control room. Harris told him he thought *Argo* had just passed over a giant boiler. They looked at the videotape from *Argo*'s cameras. Sure enough, it was a huge, round boiler that had been used to make steam to drive a ship's engines. They could hardly believe their eyes and replayed the tape to be sure. But was the boiler from *Titanic*?

TITANIC EXPEDITION CREW MEMBERS CELEBRATE FINDING THE SUNKEN LUXURY LINER.

Ballard and Michel looked at their maps. They knew that no other ship had sunk in the area. They checked their diagrams of *Titanic*'s engine room. It had to be *Titanic*.

Everyone in the control room began to cheer. Ballard and Michel congratulated their crew. They returned to watching the monitor. More pieces of wreckage appeared on the screen. Some were so large that Lange had to raise *Argo* to avoid them.

Crew members who were not on duty heard the cheering. They rushed in to see what was happening. The control room was suddenly filled with people. This could be the moment they had all been waiting for. They watched the monitors and saw twisted steel plates, portholes, and a piece of railing. Then a huge section of the great ship appeared. Because of the size and position of the wreckage on the bottom of the sea, Ballard and Michel knew they had succeeded. The *Titanic* had been found.[6]

Ballard led his crew outside to the back deck of the *Knorr*. The moon was bright in the sky. The weather was calm, as it had been the night the *Titanic* went down. They looked at the clock. It was just after two in the morning, almost the exact time the great ship had sunk so many years before. "I really don't have much to say," Ballard said. "But I thought we might just observe a few moments of silence."[7]

Everyone stood quietly for ten minutes. They thought about the people who had died when the ship disappeared beneath the calm ocean surface. They thought about the survivors. And they thought about the lost ship.

Titanic began its short life at the Harland & Wolff Shipyard in Ireland. Ballard and Michel had brought the flag of the shipyard with them on their search for the ship. They wanted to honor *Titanic*'s birthplace when the wreck was found. One of the *Knorr*'s officers raised the Harland & Wolff flag.[8]

Titanic had given up one of its secrets. But what had caused the greatest ship ever built to sink so quickly? Robert Ballard and Jean-Louis Michel were determined to find out.

CHAPTER 2

The *Sinking* of *Titanic*

Titanic was 883 feet (269 meters) long, about the length of three football fields. It was 92.5 feet (28 meters) wide and 65 feet (20 meters) high. It had three huge propellers. Its top speed was about 25 miles (40 kilometers) per hour. At the time of its launching, *Titanic* was the biggest moving object ever built by humans.[1]

Harland & Wolff began work on the *Titanic* on March 31, 1909. More than 14,000 people worked for over two years to build the *Titanic* and its sister ship, *Olympic*.[2] More than 100,000 people watched the launching ceremony on May 31, 1911.[3]

THE *OLYMPIC* (LEFT) AND *TITANIC* (RIGHT) AT BELFAST. FOURTEEN THOUSAND PEOPLE SPENT OVER TWO YEARS BUILDING THESE SISTER SHIPS.

The *Titanic* was not completely finished when it was launched. Workers still had to build and decorate the cabins and the rest of the interior of the ship, which took an additional ten months. Finally, on March 31, 1912, *Titanic* was ready for its first voyage. At the time, it was the most elegant ship afloat.

Luxury Liner

Titanic was huge, but it was also the most modern, comfortable ship ever. It could carry 3,533 passengers and crew. (*Titanic* was not full when it sailed on its first voyage.) The passengers traveled in three classes. First class had grand dining rooms, luxurious cabins, and a swimming pool. The ship was as splendid and comfortable as an elegant hotel. *Titanic* had three elevators to take passengers between decks. It also had a grand staircase. Its first-class cabins and passageways had thick carpets. *Titanic* even carried an orchestra.

On its first voyage, many rich and famous people traveled in first-class cabins aboard *Titanic*. Most of the upper decks of the ship were reserved for first-class passengers only. Second-class passengers had lavish but smaller rooms. Third-class passengers paid the least for their tickets. Their cabins and dining rooms were smaller, and they had less

PASSENGERS STROLL ALONG THE UPPER DECK OF *TITANIC*.

space on deck for walking around. But they were still aboard the greatest ship ever built.[4]

Titanic Sails for New York

April 10, 1912, was a gusty spring day in Southampton, England. *Titanic* was ready to sail. Thousands of people lined the waterfront. At noon, Captain Edward Smith gave the order to cast off the lines that held the ship to the dock.

Titanic's gangway doors closed and its mighty engines came to life. Tiny tugboats guided the huge black-and-white ship into the Itchen River. Horns blew. The crowds cheered. The greatest ocean liner of its time set sail on its first voyage.

Disaster almost struck before *Titanic* even left the river. It sailed slowly past another ocean liner named *New York*, which was tied to the dock. The pull of *Titanic*'s propellers in the water sucked the *New York* from the dock. The *New York*'s mooring lines broke! The tugboats saved the two ships from a collision.

It was a strange coincidence that *Titanic* almost hit the *New York*. *Titanic* was going to New York City on its voyage! First, though, it stopped in Cherbourg, France, to pick up more passengers. Then it stopped in Queenstown, Ireland, to pick up its final passengers. Finally, *Titanic* headed toward the Atlantic Ocean and its destiny.

On the first day, Captain Smith did not run *Titanic* at full speed. On the second day, though, the weather was good. Everything on the great ship was working perfectly. Smith increased *Titanic*'s speed.

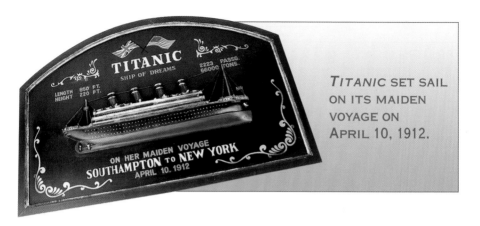

TITANIC SET SAIL
ON ITS MAIDEN
VOYAGE ON
APRIL 10, 1912.

The Iceberg's Journey

Icebergs are huge chunks of ice and rock. They float like ice cubes in a glass of water. Some icebergs are as large as ships. Others are larger than the state of Delaware. Only 10 percent of an iceberg sticks up above the water. The rest of it is hidden beneath the water's surface.

Icebergs break off from enormous, slow-moving rivers of ice called glaciers. A glacier is made of snow that hardens into solid ice. The force of gravity pulls the ice downward from higher land. Glaciers flow from mountains to the sea, where pieces break off to form icebergs. The icebergs are driven by wind and water currents out into the open sea.

About two years before *Titanic* sailed for New York, an iceberg broke off a glacier in Greenland.[5] Greenland is a big island that is almost completely covered with ice. It is on the northwest edge of the Atlantic Ocean.

The iceberg fell off the front of the glacier with a loud crack. The whole iceberg may have been 1,000 feet (300 meters) high. The part of the iceberg that was out of the water was probably about 100 feet (30 meters) high. The whole thing weighed over 300,000 tons. By the night of April 14, the iceberg was right in the path of *Titanic*.[6]

Titanic Hits the Iceberg

At 11:40 P.M. on April 14, *Titanic*'s passengers were finished with dinner. It was cold outside, so only a few were strolling on deck. Many had already gone to their cabins to sleep. Everyone felt very safe. The newspapers had proclaimed *Titanic* to be unsinkable, and everyone believed them. The great ship steamed through the darkness with starlit skies overhead. It was going 25 miles (40 kilometers) per hour.

The officers in charge of *Titanic* that night had been warned about icebergs by other ships. Captain Smith posted two lookouts near the front of the ship. The lookouts were Fred Fleet and Reginald Lee, who had come on duty at 10:00 P.M. They peered into the darkness and looked for signs of icebergs.[7]

The officers and crew on duty steered *Titanic* and communicated with the engine room from a part of the ship called the bridge. Captain Smith was in his cabin taking a short rest. First Officer William Murdoch was in charge of the ship. He was responsible for telling the sailor at the wheel what course to steer.

Suddenly Fred Fleet cried out, "Iceberg ahead! Iceberg ahead!" He rang the warning bell three times. Then he

THE MIGHTY *TITANIC* SAILED AMONG A FIELD OF ICEBERGS.

picked up the telephone to warn the bridge. "Iceberg, right ahead," he said to Officer Murdoch.[8]

"Hard to starboard!" called Murdoch. The sailor threw the wheel to the right. "Stop. Full speed astern!" Murdoch cried out. Another sailor sent that order down to the engine room.[9]

Titanic continued to speed toward the iceberg. Then gradually the ship began to turn to port. It shuddered a little as the engines went into reverse. For a moment it looked like *Titanic* would miss the iceberg.

Then disaster struck. The huge submerged portion of the iceberg collided with *Titanic's* underwater steel plates. The iceberg slid along the starboard side of the ship. It made a dull sound as it scraped past. Ice fell onto *Titanic's* forward deck. The iceberg passed behind the ship and into the night.

Then there was silence.

Titanic Is Doomed

Captain Smith rushed to the bridge and asked what had happened. Murdoch told him they had just hit an iceberg. Smith ordered another of his officers to find out if the iceberg had damaged the ship.

Titanic was divided into sixteen separate compartments. They were joined by doors that could be closed to seal off damaged compartments. If part of the ship had a hole in it, the other sections would stay dry if the watertight doors were closed. *Titanic* would then stay afloat.[10]

The news was bad. All four of *Titanic's* forward compartments were flooding with water. Captain Smith talked to the ship's chief engineer, Joseph Bell. It was determined that the ship could stay afloat for only one or two hours. The passengers must be put into lifeboats immediately. *Titanic* was doomed.[11]

Captain Smith knew one more bit of very bad news. There were only enough lifeboats for less than half the people aboard.

Titanic Goes to Its Grave

Captain Smith ordered the radio operator to send the distress signal CQD. That was the code for a ship in danger of sinking. (Today *SOS* is used instead.) If ships nearby heard that code on their radios they must hurry to help the doomed ship. CQD was the most dreaded code a sailor could send or hear. The radio operator sent out CQD. *Titanic* was sinking.

Then Captain Smith gave the order for women and children to get in the lifeboats first. During the first hour after he gave the order, many passengers thought there was no real danger. Many were not willing to get into the lifeboats. Some boats were lowered to the ocean partly full. Other lifeboats filled up.

When all the lifeboats were gone, panic swept through *Titanic*. Hundreds of people jumped into the ocean wearing life jackets. Only six of them would survive in the icy water.

THE *TITANIC* SINKS IN THE EARLY MORNING HOURS OF APRIL 15, 1912.

Many others stayed with the ship. They were swept into the sea or dragged to the bottom with *Titanic*.[12]

By 2:20 A.M., *Titanic* was gone. The bow of the ship sank first. The stern stayed afloat for a few more minutes. Then it went down, too.

The 712 survivors were picked up a few hours later by another ocean liner, the SS *Carpathia*. Hundreds of others who had gone into the water in life jackets or clinging to wreckage died before the rescue ship arrived.[13]

CHAPTER 3

Exploring *Titanic*

*itanic* rested alone in its watery grave for over seven decades. No human eyes had seen the lost ship until Robert Ballard and Jean-Louis Michel located it in 1985. *Titanic* lay in two big pieces on the bottom not far from where it sank. The wreck was 1,300 miles (2,093 kilometers) east of New York and 400 miles (644 kilometers) southeast of the island of Newfoundland. *Titanic*'s grave was 12,400 feet (3,780 meters) beneath the surface of the sea.[1]

In 1986, Ballard returned to explore the *Titanic*. Jean-Louis Michel did not come on this second expedition. Michel would lead other expeditions in following years. On July 12, Ballard arrived over *Titanic*'s grave on his research ship *Atlantis II*.[2]

This time, Ballard would dive to *Titanic* in *Alvin*. *Alvin* is a little submarine that can carry three people. It has spotlights and windows for exploring the deep sea. With *Alvin*, Ballard hoped he would actually see *Titanic* with his own eyes. Exploring *Titanic* had been Robert Ballard's dream since he was very young. Thanks to *Alvin*, his dream could come true. And he hoped to solve the mystery of how *Titanic* sank.

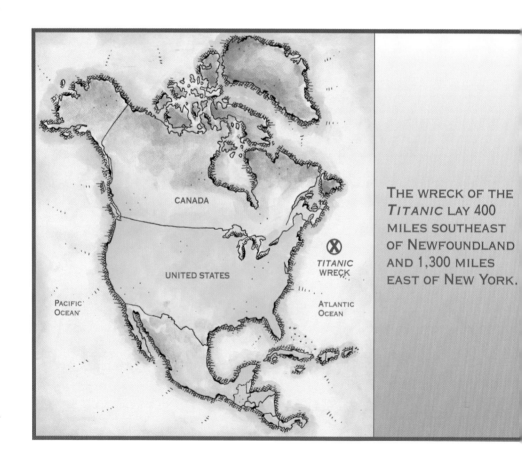

THE WRECK OF THE *TITANIC* LAY 400 MILES SOUTHEAST OF NEWFOUNDLAND AND 1,300 MILES EAST OF NEW YORK.

Alvin and *Jason Jr.*

Alvin is made of titanium, a metal much stronger than steel. *Alvin* can move forward and backward and dive to a depth of 14,764 feet (4,500 meters). That's almost three miles below the surface of the ocean. *Alvin* could reach the *Titanic*.³

Alvin carried a small robot submarine, *Jason Jr.* This was a brand-new kind of remotely operated vehicle (ROV). *Jason Jr.* was connected to *Alvin* with a cable called a tether. The little robot could send pictures from its television cameras through the tether to *Alvin*. Ballard would use *Jason Jr.* to explore the inside of *Titanic*.

A pilot inside *Alvin* controlled *Jason Jr.* He used a joystick to move the robot. He could turn the lights and cameras on and off. Everyone was excited about using the small robot. They wanted to visit inside *Titanic*'s cabins, dining rooms, and other places on the lost ship. No one had ever done anything like this before.⁴

Diving to *Titanic*

Robert Ballard and his crew had prepared for almost a year for exploring *Titanic*. Finally the day of the first dive arrived. The crew rolled *Alvin* from its hangar on the deck of *Atlantis II*. Robert Ballard, pilot Ralph Hollis, and copilot Dudley Foster prepared for the first descent. They took off their shoes and climbed into the tiny cabin.

Hollis closed *Alvin*'s hatch. Ballard turned on the oxygen tank. Outside, a winch on *Atlantis II*'s deck lifted *Alvin* up

INSIDE THE SUBMERSIBLE *ALVIN*, ROBERT BALLARD AND HIS PILOT AND COPILOT DROPPED TO THE OCEAN DEPTHS IN SEARCH OF THE *TITANIC* WRECK.

and over the stern. The winch slowly lowered *Alvin* into the water. Three divers swam around the submersible and made final checks for the dive. At 8:35 A.M., the controller on *Atlantis II* told *Alvin* it was cleared to dive. Next stop, *Titanic*.

The men huddled in the cramped cabin. Hollis threw a switch to flood *Alvin*'s tanks with water and begin the descent. As the sub slipped beneath the surface, Ballard watched a jellyfish drift past the window. Then he saw a shark swim by. The shark was curious about the strange machine entering its domain, but it left the contraption alone.

The first dive was a test. Ballard wanted to see if he could safely get close to *Titanic*. *Jason Jr.* would stay in its garage aboard *Alvin*. The little robot would be used to explore *Titanic* beginning with the second dive.

Diving into the deep ocean is always dangerous. The water put enormous pressure on *Alvin*'s hull. Outside, the water was nearly freezing, and the cabin grew colder as they descended. The men put on more clothes to keep warm. The dive to *Titanic* would take two and a half hours.

On the way to the bottom, the men relaxed and looked out the windows. They played music on the stereo system. Fifteen minutes after they began the descent, the sea was totally black. No sunlight reaches the deep ocean. The light inside *Alvin* was soft red. The dials and gauges glowed. Down, down they went.

First Sight of *Titanic*

The controller on *Atlantis II* directed *Alvin* to *Titanic*. Ballard switched on powerful searchlights. They crawled along the bottom but saw nothing. The men strained their eyes at the viewing ports. Still there was nothing. An alarm sounded. Some of *Alvin*'s batteries were not working very well. Hollis said they would have to surface soon.

Just then the seafloor began to look strange. It sloped upward at a steep angle. Ballard's heartbeat quickened. "Come right," he said to Hollis. "I think I see a wall of black just on the other side of that mud mound."[5]

Suddenly, a dark steel wall towered over tiny *Alvin*. Ballard, Hollis, and Foster gasped. There it was. *Titanic*. Through the murky water, the ship looked enormous. For the first time in seventy-four years, human eyes could see the most famous ship in history.

The battery alarm continued to sound. Hollis told Ballard they must return to the surface immediately. They were in no danger, but he did not want to risk harming the sub. After just two minutes with *Titanic*, they began their ascent. Ballard was disappointed. He had not been able to explore at all. But he knew he would dive again the next day.[6]

A Closer Look at *Titanic*

The next day, Ballard and Hollis prepared to descend again to *Titanic*. The third crew member was Martin Bowen, who was an expert at piloting *Jason Jr.* Again, they made the long dive to the bottom.

This time, *Alvin* performed perfectly. Ballard's second view of *Titanic* was breathtaking. As they glided along the bottom, the sharp edge of the ship's high bow loomed ahead. Ballard saw the two huge anchors still in their places. He saw

THE BOW OF THE *TITANIC* WAS COVERED IN RUSTY COLUMNS, WHICH BALLARD NAMED RUSTICLES.

that the bow had driven deeply into the mud when it made its deadly dive.

Hollis guided *Alvin* along the side of the ship. Everything was covered with rust. Some of the rust formed long columns like icicles. Ballard named these formations rusticles. Crabs and sea worms were living all over the wreck. All the wood on the ship had been eaten away. The explorers could clearly see rails, one of the ship's cranes, and the remains of the bridge. The wooden wheelhouse had completely vanished.

They rose above *Titanic*'s deck to look for a place to land. Ballard knew that the glass dome that had once covered the grand first-class staircase would give them an opening into *Titanic*. He particularly wanted to see the staircase.

Emergency on the Bottom

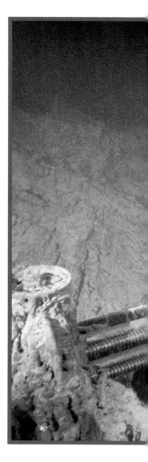

They had been on the bottom for almost two hours. Hollis was piloting *Alvin* along the upper deck when disaster struck. The crew felt a thump. The sub shuddered and clanged. A shower of rust covered the windows. "Ralph, we've hit something," Ballard said.[7]

Hollis carefully backed up. They saw what they had hit. It was a davit, a curved pole used for hanging a lifeboat on a ship. They continued to rise. The current was very strong and Hollis had trouble steering. Ballard saw that they were headed for a tangle of wreckage on the deck.

"Swing back to the left," Ballard cried. "I have wreckage just out of my view port and it's getting close. Swing left!"

"It won't come around into the current," Hollis answered.

This was the worst nightmare for a deep diver. They were out of control near tangled steel and cables that could trap them forever.

THIS MAGNIFICENT UNDERWATER PHOTOGRAPH INCLUDES THE TIP OF THE TOPPLED FORWARD MAST FROM *TITANIC*.

"Then come up," Ballard said. "Let's get out of here! It's too dangerous." For a few long seconds, *Alvin* failed to respond to Hollis's commands. Then slowly it rose away from the wreckage.[8]

The controller on *Atlantis II* told them that the weather on the surface was getting bad. Picking up *Alvin* in rough seas is very difficult. Every minute more they spent on the bottom meant more danger. Just then, the battery alarm began to sound again. This dive was over.

Hollis made one more pass along *Titanic*'s side. Then the long ascent began. Ballard played music on the stereo. The men tried to relax. They had had a close call, but everything was okay. When they arrived on the surface, the sea was very stormy. *Jason Jr.* accidentally slipped out of its garage, but divers rescued it. Finally, *Alvin* was safe in its cradle.

The crew of *Atlantis II* crowded into the video studio. Ballard showed them the videotapes of the dive. They saw the great bow planted in the mud. They saw the decks, the portholes, and the remains of the bridge. Everyone was stunned as they viewed *Titanic* in its grave.

RMS *Titanic*

LENGTH: 883 feet (269 meters)

WIDTH: 92.5 feet (28 meters)

HEIGHT ABOVE WATER: 65 feet (20 meters)

WEIGHT: 46,328 tons (42,040 metric tons)

TOP SPEED: 25 miles (40 kilometers) per hour

BUILDER: Harland & Wolff Shipyard, Belfast, Ireland

BUILDING BEGAN: March 31, 1909

LAUNCHED: May 31, 1911

COMPLETED: March 31, 1912

FIRST VOYAGE: April 10, 1912

PASSENGER AND CREW CAPACITY: 3,533

PASSENGERS AND CREW (FIRST VOYAGE): 2,209

LOST AT SEA: 1,497

SURVIVORS: 712

DISCOVERED BY: Robert Ballard and Jean-Louis Michel
September 1, 1985

DEPTH OF GRAVE: 12,400 feet (3,780 meters)

First-class bedrooms (top), a gymnasium (top right), cafés (right), and the grand staircase were some of the features that made *Titanic* the most luxurious ship of its time.

CHAPTER 4

Inside
Titanic

Robert Ballard and his crew had seen many photographs of *Titanic*. Hundreds of pictures of the ship had been taken before it sailed on its fateful voyage. Some cabins had fine furniture, fireplaces, and bathtubs. The walls were covered with silk. All the wood was perfectly painted and polished. Passengers could enjoy a steam room, several cafés and dining rooms, a swimming pool, and a barber shop.

The most beautiful feature of *Titanic* was its grand staircase. This connected the first-class passenger deck with the dining room. The staircase was lit at night by gold-plated chandeliers. During the day, sunlight shone down through a huge glass dome.[1]

Ballard knew the glass dome had shattered when the ship sank. He planned to land *Alvin* on the deck near the hole where the glass dome had been. From there, he would send *Jason Jr.* down into the hole and then into the hallways, rooms, and cabins. With the little robot, Ballard would bring the long lost *Titanic* to life again.

Jason Jr. Descends the Staircase

Dudley Foster piloted *Alvin* to a landing on *Titanic*'s deck. The hole where the glass dome had been was straight ahead. Ballard asked Foster to get as close to the edge as he could. Slowly, *Alvin* crept forward. The men heard the whirring of the thrusters. Then silence.

They were in perfect position to send *Jason Jr.* into *Titanic*. Martin Bowen sat with the control box for *Jason Jr.* on his lap. He commanded the robot to leave its garage on the front of *Alvin*. He piloted it out a few feet. Then he turned it around to face *Alvin*. The first pictures on the monitor from *Jason Jr.* were of *Alvin* on the deck of *Titanic*.[2]

The crew called *Jason Jr.* "*JJ*" for short. The little sub cost a half million dollars. No one wanted to lose it. But if *JJ* got tangled up or trapped, Bowen could cut the tether to free *Alvin* and its crew. Otherwise, *Alvin* would be trapped, too.

JJ floated out over the staircase. From there it began to descend into the ship. Bowen kept the robot close to the side of the staircase. The only thing the men in *Alvin* could see on the monitor was the rusty orange wall. Then *JJ* was at the bottom of the staircase.

PART OF *TITANIC*'S GRAND STAIRCASE RESTS AT THE BOTTOM OF THE OCEAN.

Ballard, Foster, and Bowen could see the dim shapes of pillars lining the room. They were shocked to see that one of the gold chandeliers was still hanging. It had survived the two-and-a-half-mile plunge to the bottom.[3]

The men imagined the last hours of *Titanic*'s fateful voyage. They imagined well-groomed men and women in formal clothes gracefully walking down the staircase for dinner. They summoned the sounds of the orchestra coming from the dining room. The *Titanic* was alive again.

BALLARD, FOSTER, AND BOWEN IMAGINED THE DAYS WHEN FORMALLY DRESSED PASSENGERS GRACED THE GRAND STAIRCASE ON THEIR WAY TO DINNER.

JJ explored for a few more minutes. Then Foster said it was time to return to the surface. Everyone wanted to stay, but rules were rules. They had stayed as long as they safely could. Bowen backed *JJ* out of the staircase. He brought the robot back to its garage on *Alvin*. The dive was a huge success.

Mystery Solved

Robert Ballard was living his dream. He had landed on *Titanic* and explored the grand staircase. He and his crew made fifteen dives that summer. On every one, *Titanic* became more real. On one dive they used *Jason Jr.* to scan the side of the ship. What they saw solved the second mystery of *Titanic*.

Using *JJ*'s cameras, they could see part of the iceberg damage on *Titanic*'s side. It looked like the iceberg had not cut a gash in the ship after all. Probably, the force of the collision had caused rivets to break. Then the plates on the side of the ship came apart at the seams. Water flooded in.[4] No ship could have survived. Later, Ballard and other explorers confirmed the theory that the steel plates had come apart.

CHAPTER 5

The Legend of *Titanic*

O n his last dive in 1986, Robert Ballard left an inscribed metal plate on *Titanic*. It honors the ship and the people who were lost on that fateful night in 1912. Ballard hoped the great ship would rest in peace.[1]

But in 1987 French divers returned to *Titanic*. A group of Americans paid for the expedition. They wanted to salvage things from the wreck and put them on display in museums. Anything from the legendary *Titanic* is very valuable.

The French divers used their own submersible *Nautile*. It had robotic arms and could pick up things from around the main wreck of the ship. They brought

When Robert Ballard made his final dive in 1986 to the *Titanic*, he placed an inscribed plaque on the ship. It included the following words: "In memory of those souls who perished with the *Titanic* April 14/15, 1912."

over 800 pieces of wreckage back to the surface. These included dishes, cups, silverware, a ship's bell, luggage, lights, and metal furniture.[2]

Many people were angry about the salvage expedition. They wanted the exploration to continue, but they did not want the wreck to be disturbed. It was really a grave for hundreds of people. One of the survivors of *Titanic* was Eva Hart. She was seven when the ship sank. When she heard about the salvage expedition, she was furious. "The grave should be left alone," she said. "They're simply going to do it as fortune hunters, vultures, pirates!"[3]

HUNDREDS OF THESE SPECIAL CLAY DISHES FROM *TITANIC* WERE RECOVERED FROM THE OCEAN BOTTOM. THE WOODEN CABINET IN WHICH THEY WERE KEPT PROTECTED THEM DURING THE SINKING. OVER TIME THE WOOD ROTTED AWAY, LEAVING THE DISHES STACKED NEATLY TOGETHER IN THE SAND. THESE PLATES ALLOWED *TITANIC*'S COOKS TO PREPARE MEALS UNDER VERY HIGH HEAT AND THEN SERVE THE SAME DISH AT THE TABLE.

After the anger about salvaging things from *Titanic*, the next visitors took no souvenirs. In 1991, a Russian and Canadian expedition dove to make a movie. They brought two submersibles with them, *Mir I* and *Mir II*. (*Mir* means "peace" in Russian.) They only brought back steel plates and rivets to test whether or not they were weak before the ship sank. The crews of *Mir I* and *Mir II* also spent 140 hours on the bottom photographing *Titanic*. The edited film was shown in IMAX theaters all over the world.[4]

Then the popular movie *Titanic* was released in 1997. It was the best picture of the year. Millions of people sat in theaters and watched the great ship sail from England. They could see its beauty and power. And they could feel the pain of its loss.

Titanic was already a legend when it sailed off to meet its fate on its first voyage. And it still is. Other deep submersibles continue to make the long dive into the darkness to *Titanic*. They are exploring deeper into its hallways, cabins, and rooms. Their passengers can look out and imagine *Titanic* when it sailed the Atlantic as the greatest ship afloat.

Everyone who knows the story of *Titanic* keeps it alive in their memories. They pay tribute to the ship and the passengers and crew that were lost at sea. Now that the wreck has been found, the story is even more unforgettable.

Chapter Notes

CHAPTER 1. SEARCHING FOR *TITANIC*

1. Söldner, Hermann, *RMS Titanic Passenger and Crew List (10 April 1912–15 April 1912)* (Ruti, Switzerland: Verlag, 2000).

2. Robert Ballard, *The Discovery of the Titanic* (Toronto: Madison Press Books, 1989), p. 11.

3. *Titanic* Discovery, *Titanic Found*, <http://www.titanic-online. com/titanic/expeditions/discovery.html> (September 10, 2002).

4. Steinar D. Varsi, *R.M.S. Titanic Is Found!*, <http://www.varsi. net/english/found.shtml> (September 10, 2002).

5. Ballard, p. 133.

6. Ibid., pp. 135–136.

7. Ibid., p. 137.

8. *Titanic* Discovery.

CHAPTER 2. THE SINKING OF *TITANIC*

1. John. P. Eaton and Charles A. Haas, *Titanic: Triumph and Tragedy* (New York: W. W. Norton & Co., 1994), p. 21.

2. Don Lynch, *Titanic: An Illustrated History* (New York: Hyperion, 1992), p. 21.

3. Eaton and Haas, p. 21.

4. Ibid., pp. 30–37.

5. Richard Brown, *Voyage of the Iceberg: The Story of the Iceberg that Sank the Titanic* (New York: Beaufort Books, 1984), pp. 15–25.

6. Ibid.

7. John P. Eaton and Charles A. Haas, *Titanic: Destination Disaster, The Legends and the Reality* (New York: W. W. Norton & Company, 1994), p. 14.

8. Ibid.

9. Ibid., p. 16.

10. Eaton and Haas, *Titanic: Triumph and Tragedy*, p. 143.

11. Lynch, p. 92.

12. Eaton and Haas, *Titanic: Triumph and Tragedy*, pp. 138–162.

13. Eaton and Haas, *Titanic: Destination Disaster, The Legends and the Reality*, pp. 45–49.

Chapter Notes

Chapter 3. Exploring *Titanic*

1. A Ti-tanic Home Page, *Where Is the Titanic?*, © 1996, <http://www.geocities.com/Athens/3104/location.html> (December 4, 2002).
2. Robert Ballard, *The Discovery of the Titanic* (Toronto: Madison Press Books, 1989), p. 165.
3. Woods Hole Oceanographic Institution, *A History of Alvin* <http://www.whoi.edu/marops/vehicles/alvin/spec_alvin.html> (August 3, 2002).
4. Ballard, pp. 165–166.
5. Ibid., p. 179.
6. Ibid., p. 180.
7. Ibid., p. 194.
8. Ibid., p. 195.

Chapter 4. Inside *Titanic*

1. Don Lynch, *Titanic: An Illustrated History* (New York: Hyperion, 1992), pp. 46–63.
2. Robert Ballard, *The Discovery of the Titanic* (Toronto: Madison Press Books, 1989), p. 202.
3. Ibid., p. 203.
4. Ibid., p. 233.

Chapter 5. The Legend of *Titanic*

1. Robert Ballard, *The Discovery of the Titanic* (Toronto: Madison Press Books, 1989), p. 232.
2. Don Lynch, *Titanic: An Illustrated History* (New York: Hyperion, 1992), pp. 205–209.
3. Ibid., p. 208.
4. Ibid., p. 209.

Glossary

boiler—Part of a ship's engine that holds water to make steam.

bow—The front of a ship.

bridge—The part of a ship where the crew steers and controls the engines.

CQD—An international telegraph code sent by a ship in distress; its use faded several years after the new code SOS was adopted in 1908.

glacier—A very slow-moving river of ice that forms when snow builds up in high areas, becomes ice, and flows downhill.

hydraulic—Powered by fluid pushed through hoses by a pump.

mooring lines—Ropes that tie a ship to a dock or other structure.

port—To the left on a ship when facing forward.

salvage—To take sunken ships or their wreckage from the ocean.

sea cucumber—An animal shaped like a cucumber that lives on the seafloor.

starboard—To the right on a ship when facing forward.

submersible—A manned research submarine that can operate without a cable to the surface because its pilots can control its buoyancy.

thruster—A small electric propeller that is used for steering a submersible.

titanium—A very strong, light metal used in building submersibles, airplanes, and other modern machinery.

Further Reading

BOOKS

Ballard, Robert. *Exploring the Titanic*. New York: Scholastic, Inc., 1998.

Brewster, Hugh. *Inside the Titanic*. Boston: Little, Brown, & Co., 1997.

Cole, Michael D. *The Titanic: Disaster at Sea*. Berkeley Heights, N.J.: Enslow Publishers, Inc., 2001.

Hill, Christine. *Robert Ballard: Oceanographer Who Discovered the Titanic*. Berkeley Heights, N.J.: Enslow Publishers, Inc., 1999.

Kentley, Eric. *Discover the Titanic*. New York: DK Publishers, 2001.

Landau, Elaine. *Heroine of the Titanic: The Real Unsinkable Molly Brown*. New York: Houghton Mifflin Co., 2001.

INTERNET ADDRESSES

RMS Titanic, Inc. *Titanic Discovery*. © 2000. <http://www.titanic-online.com/titanic/expeditions/discovery.html>

The Titanic Historical Society, Inc. n.d. <http://www.titanic1.org/>

Woods Hole Oceanographic Institution. *Dive and Discover.* © 2002. <http://www.divediscover.whoi.edu/about.html>

Index